SPORTS SUPERSTARS

JOSE ALTUVE

By Anthony K. Hewson

I0895880

Kaleidoscope
Minneapolis, MN

Your Front Row Seat to the Games

This edition is co-published by agreement between Kaleidoscope and World Book, Inc.

Kaleidoscope Publishing, Inc.
6012 Blue Circle Drive
Minnetonka, MN 55343 U.S.A.

World Book, Inc.
180 North LaSalle St., Suite 900
Chicago IL 60601 U.S.A.

All rights reserved. No part of this book may be reproduced in any form without written permission from the publishers.

Kaleidoscope ISBNs
978-1-64519-038-7 (library bound)
978-1-64494-196-6 (paperback)
978-1-64519-139-1 (ebook)

World Book ISBN
978-0-7166-4341-8 (library bound)

Library of Congress Control Number
2019940058

Text copyright ©2020 by Kaleidoscope Publishing, Inc.
All-Star Sports, Bigfoot Books, and associated logos are trademarks and/or registered trademarks of Kaleidoscope Publishing, Inc.

Printed in the United States of America.

TABLE OF CONTENTS

CHAPTER 1

Game 2 Hero

Jose Altuve smiled. He was seated next to greatness. To his right was Hank Aaron. Only one Major League Baseball (MLB) player had hit more career home runs than Aaron. Now Altuve was receiving an award. It was named after Aaron. The award goes to the best offensive player in each major league. Altuve won the 2017 award for the American League (AL).

Altuve wore his Houston Astros uniform. Spelled out in orange and blue was "HOUSTON" across his chest. Houston, Texas, had become his home. He played his hardest for the city. Altuve was thinking about the fans back home. They were getting ready to watch him play. That's because the second baseman's day was only just beginning.

Hank Aaron

Jose Altuve accepts the 2017 AL Hank Aaron Award.

The Astros were in the 2017 World Series. Game 2 began in one hour. Houston trailed the Los Angeles Dodgers. A win would even up the series.

Altuve had a tough game. He struck out twice. But his teammates picked him up. They **rallied** to tie the game in the ninth. That meant **extra innings**.

Altuve led off the tenth inning. He had been impatient earlier in the game. Usually he had a good eye. He would wait for a good pitch. But Altuve kept swinging early. Now he took a pitch outside. Ball one. He took another. Outside again, ball two. Then he didn't have to wait any longer. Altuve got his pitch.

Altuve finally got the pitch he was looking for in the tenth inning.

CAREER STATS

Through the 2018 season

BATTING AVERAGE	.316
HITS	1,419
RUNS BATTED IN (RBIs)	464
HOME RUNS	97

It was a fastball. The pitch flew right over the middle of the plate. Altuve turned on the ball, driving all of his weight forward. The ball soared out above left center field. It landed in the first row of the stands. Home run!

The Astros went on to win. That tied the World Series. Winning the Hank Aaron Award showed that Altuve was a great player. Then he went out and proved it. A few days later, his Astros won the World Series.

EXTRA POWER

Altuve was one of three Astros to homer in extra innings. Carlos Correa and George Springer hit the others. The Dodgers also hit two homers. The five home runs in extra innings set a playoffs record.

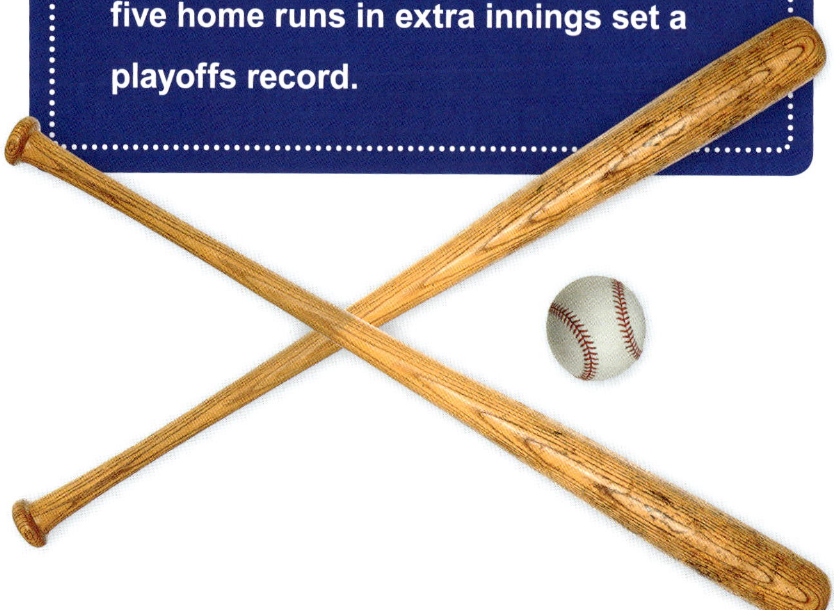

Carlos Correa, right, congratulates Altuve on his big home run.

CHAPTER 2

Getting a Chance

Jose Altuve stepped onto a dusty baseball field in 2006. He stretched in the Venezuelan sun. He was ready. He had played the sport for most of his 16 years. Now he would show off his skills.

Several other players warmed up with him. Watching them were Houston Astros **scouts**. This was an MLB tryout. Jose's big-league dreams started there.

But they almost ended that quickly. Jose was short. The scouts sent him home. He did not even get to show how he could play.

FUN FACT

The shortest MLB player ever, Eddie Gaedel, stood just 3-foot-7 (1.1 m). He played in just one game in 1951.

Nothing was guaranteed in Jose's baseball journey.

FUN FACT

More than 30 players from Jose's hometown of Maracay have reached the major leagues.

Altuve plays for the Venezuela national team at the 2017 World Baseball Classic.

Jose went home and told his dad. Carlos Altuve had taught his son how to play. And he was the one to tell Jose not to take no for an answer. Jose went back to the tryout the next day.

One of the scouts was named Al Pedrique. He had worked in baseball for a long time.

Pedrique watched Jose play. His defense needed work. And yes, he was short. But Pedrique believed in him. Jose was confident.

“Can you play?” Pedrique asked him.

“I’ll show you,” Jose replied.

Where Altuve Has Been

1 **Puerto Cabello, Venezuela:** Altuve was born here.

2 **Maracay, Venezuela:** This is Altuve's hometown.

3 **Guacara, Venezuela:** Altuve made his pro baseball debut in the Venezuelan Summer League.

4 **Tusculum, Tennessee:** Altuve played with the Greeneville Astros after moving to the United States.

5 **Troy, New York:** Altuve played with the Tri-City ValleyCats.

6 **Lexington, Kentucky:** Altuve played with the Lexington Legends.

7 **Lancaster, California:** Altuve played with the Lancaster JetHawks.

8 **Corpus Christi, Texas:** Altuve played with the Corpus Christi Hooks.

9 **Houston, Texas:** Altuve's current home is with the Astros.

Pedrique pushed the Astros to sign Jose. He told them about the kid with the quick bat. He talked about how fast he was. The Astros were convinced. They offered Jose a **contract**. It was worth $15,000. Jose did not care about the money.

"I will sign the contract," Jose said. "I just want a chance."

And he got it. The next year, he started playing in the **minor leagues**. At first, his manager did not want to play him. He was too small. Other teams didn't believe he could hit, either. They threw him easy pitches. Jose crushed them. Fielders moved in, thinking he was weak. Jose lined balls over their heads. By the end of the season, he was playing every day. He was well on his way to the majors.

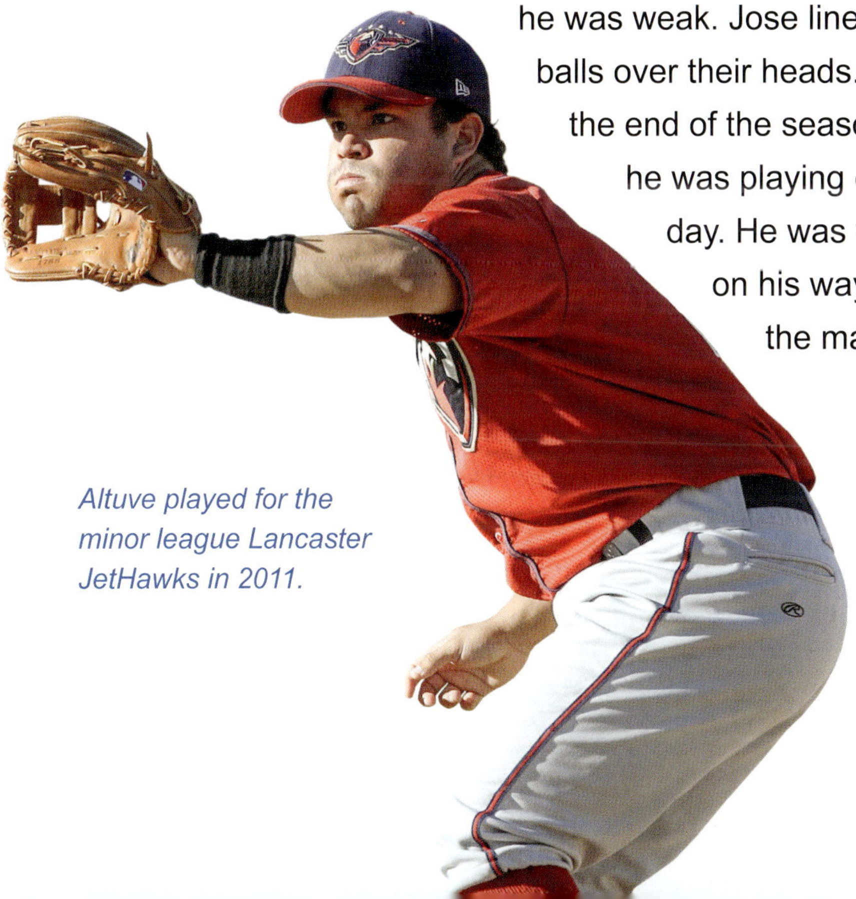

Altuve played for the minor league Lancaster JetHawks in 2011.

CHAPTER 3

Tuve

Jose Altuve steps into the **batter's box**. All eyes are on him. He feels the pressure. The pitcher looks in. He knows about Altuve. The Astros' slugger has won three batting titles. Now the pitcher has to fool him.

The pitch comes in. It's high. Altuve swings wildly. He hits only air. The pitcher wins this time. But Altuve just smiles. This is not an MLB game. He is not even in the United States. He is back home in Venezuela. He has joined some kids in a game of **stickball**.

FUN FACT

No major publication listed Jose as a top-100 **prospect**.

Altuve is known for being a great teammate.

Altuve remembered when he got his first glove. It was so special to have one of his own. He wanted other kids to experience that. In 2018, Altuve held a camp for kids in the United States. While learning about the game, they also donated gloves for kids in Venezuela. Altuve then brought the gloves there on one of his trips home.

FUN FACT

Altuve's first child, a daughter named Melanie Andrea, was born in October 2016.

ALTUVES

Altuve stands just 5 feet, 6 inches (1.7 m) tall. That makes him the shortest player in baseball. One fan took that to the extreme. He made a site to calculate distance in "Altuves." The distance from home plate to first base? That's 90 feet (27.4 m). Or that's 16.6 Altuves.

"Everything I can do to help my country, I'm going to be really happy to do it," Altuve said.

Altuve leads a group of kids in a baseball clinic in San Joaquin, Venezuela.

Altuve's play and community work have helped him become a fan favorite in Houston.

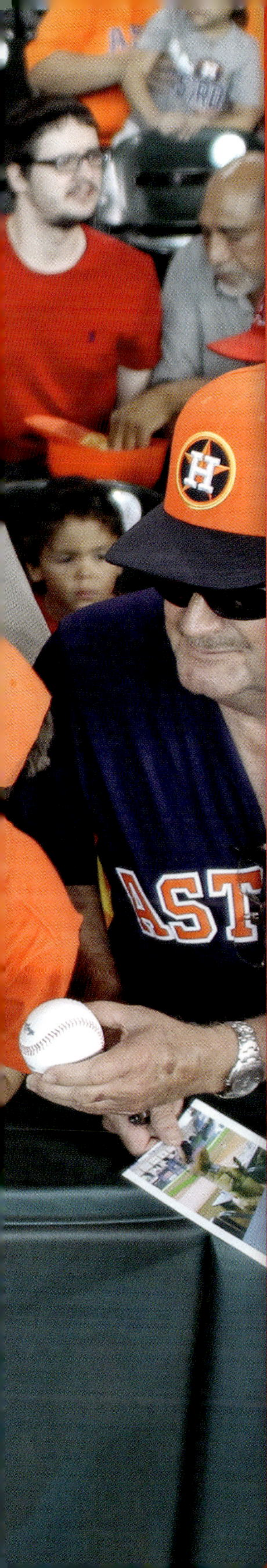

Venezuela will always be Altuve's home. But Houston has become his home, too. In 2017, Hurricane Harvey damaged the city. Altuve donated money and time to help. He gave $30,000. He also donated clothes to people in need.

Altuve also helped with his play. The Astros reached the World Series that year. He helped boost the city's spirits. The magazine *Sports Illustrated* named him a Sportsperson of the Year.

"The city of Houston has treated me really good since I got to the big leagues," Altuve said. "And I felt that I owed them something."

Houston, Texas

CHAPTER 4

Houston's MVP

Altuve lifted the helmet off his head. Then he saluted a fan behind home plate. Altuve had just hit a double. It was his 210th hit of the 2014 season. That tied a team record set by Craig Biggio. Seated behind the plate, Biggio clapped.

FUN FACT
One of Altuve's favorite workouts involves slamming a sledgehammer into a giant tire.

Altuve came up again in the seventh. This time he lined a single up the middle. The **dugout** erupted in cheers. Biggio stood and applauded. So did everyone else. Now the record was Altuve's.

However, the Astros lost the game. It was their 84th defeat of the season. And only 18,000 fans were there to watch. Altuve was one of baseball's best young hitters. But the Astros struggled.

Altuve tips his cap after setting the Astros' single-season hit record in 2014.

Altuve stayed loyal. By 2017, the Astros were in the World Series. And Altuve was a superstar. He led the AL in hitting with a .346 batting average. But he was struggling in the World Series.

Still, he managed some big hits. In Game 5, the Astros trailed the Dodgers 7–4. Two Astros were on base. The home crowd was roaring. Altuve worked a **full count**. Then came a fastball. It was right down the middle. Altuve hammered it to left center field. It went into the second deck for a home run. The game was tied 7–7.

Altuve blasts a three-run homer in Game 5 of the 2017 World Series.

CAREER TIMELINE

1990

May 6, 1990
Altuve is born in Puerto Cabello, Venezuela.

2006

2006
Altuve attends an Astros tryout camp in Venezuela. He signs his first pro baseball contract.

2007

2007
Altuve makes his pro baseball debut in the Venezuelan Summer League.

2008

2008
Altuve moves to the United States and begins playing with the Greeneville Astros.

2011

July 20, 2011
Altuve makes his major-league debut with the Houston Astros.

2012

2012
Altuve plays in his first MLB All-Star Game.

2014

2014
Altuve wins his first AL batting title with a .341 average.

2016

2016
Altuve wins his second AL batting title with a .338 average.

2017

2017
Altuve wins the AL Most Valuable Player (MVP) Award and leads the Astros to their first World Series title.

2018

2018
Altuve makes his sixth All-Star Game and hits at least .300 for the fifth season in a row.

Altuve came up again in the seventh. A runner was on. And now the game was tied 8–8. This time Altuve drove the ball to deep left center. It went over the left fielder's head for a double. Houston took the lead. Altuve was keeping his team alive.

The Astros won that game. They went on to win the World Series. Altuve won the AL MVP Award. One year later Altuve led Houston back to the playoffs. The losing days were over. And Altuve was still a star.

FUN FACT

Founded in 1962, the Astros had been to just one World Series—and lost—prior to 2017.

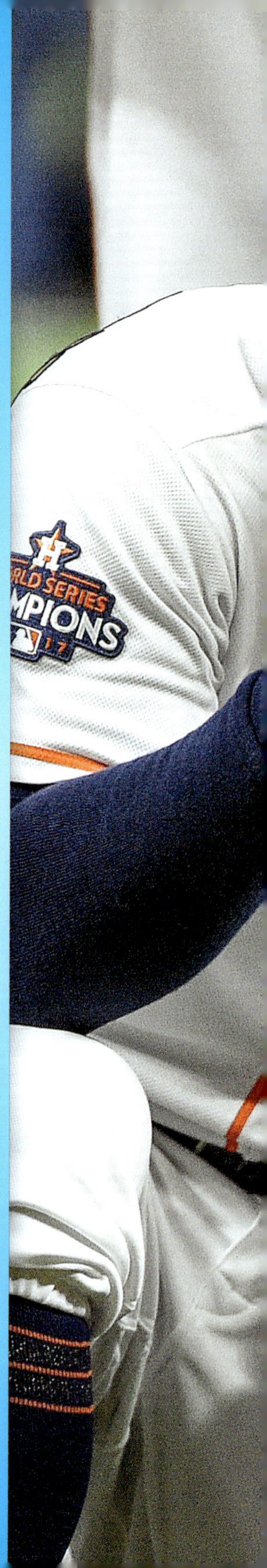

Altuve, center, shows off his World Series ring with Alex Bregman, left, and Carlos Correa.

BEYOND THE BOOK

After reading the book, it's time to think about what you learned. Try the following exercises to jumpstart your ideas.

THINK

THAT'S NEWS TO ME. Chapter One describes Altuve's big hit in Game 2 of the 2017 World Series. What news sources would have covered this event? What new information might these sources have? Where would you find sources like that?

CREATE

SHARPEN YOUR RESEARCH SKILLS. Where would you go in the library to find out more about Altuve? Who could you talk to? Make a research plan of how you'd go about finding this information. Write a paragraph describing the steps.

SHARE

WHAT'S YOUR OPINION? Chapter Four states that Craig Biggio is an important player in Astros history. What evidence is given to support this opinion? What other evidence can you find to agree or disagree with it? Present this opinion and evidence to a friend. Did your friend find the argument convincing?

GROW

REAL-LIFE RESEARCH. This book contains a lot of facts and achievements from Altuve's career. But there are more ways to learn about a subject than by reading about them. What real places could you go that would tell you more about Altuve? What else could you learn at these places?

RESEARCH NINJA

Visit www.ninjaresearcher.com/0387 to learn how to take your research skills and book report writing to the next level!

RESEARCH

DIGITAL LITERACY TOOLS

SEARCH LIKE A PRO

Learn about how to use search engines to find useful websites.

FACT OR FAKE?

Discover how you can tell a trusted website from an untrustworthy resource.

TEXT DETECTIVE

Explore how to zero in on the information you need most.

SHOW YOUR WORK

Research responsibly—learn how to cite sources.

WRITE

GET TO THE POINT

Learn how to express your main ideas.

PLAN OF ATTACK

Learn prewriting exercises and create an outline.

DOWNLOADABLE REPORT FORMS

Further Resources

BOOKS

Abdo, Kenny. *Jose Altuve*. Abdo Publishing, 2018.

Fishman, Jon M. *Jose Altuve*. Lerner Publications, 2018.

Flynn, Brendan. *Superstars of the World Series*. Pop!, 2018.

WEBSITES

FACTSURFER

Factsurfer.com gives you a safe, fun way to find more information.

1. Go to www.factsurfer.com.
2. Enter "Jose Altuve" into the search box and click .
3. Select your book cover to see a list of related websites.

Glossary

batter's box: The batter's box is an outlined area next to home plate where a hitter stands while hitting. Altuve stepped into the batter's box.

contract: A contract is a legal agreement between two parties, such as a player and a team. Altuve signed a contract to play for the Astros.

dugout: A dugout is an area below the playing field where players sit. Altuve went back to the dugout after hitting.

extra innings: Baseball games that are tied after nine innings go to extra innings. The Astros beat the Dodgers in extra innings.

full count: Hitters face a full count when they have three balls and two strikes against them. Altuve hit a home run on a full count.

minor leagues: Minor leagues are lower levels of competition where baseball players develop their skills. Altuve began his pro career in the minor leagues.

prospect: A prospect is a baseball player who has potential to make the major leagues. Altuve was never a top prospect.

rallied: A team that came back to win a game rallied from a deficit. The Astros rallied to win over the Dodgers.

scouts: Scouts are team employees who evaluate future players. Scouts took notice of Altuve's skills during a tryout.

stickball: Stickball is a casual form of baseball that kids play using a thinner bat and any ball they can find. Many kids in Venezuela grow up playing stickball.

Index

PHOTO CREDITS

The images in this book are reproduced through the courtesy of: Albert Pena/Cal Sport Media/ AP Images, front cover (center); Alex Gallardo/AP Images, front cover (right), pp. 3, 5; EFKS/ Shutterstock Images, front cover (background top); Marcio Jose Bastos Silva/Shutterstock Images, front cover (background bottom); AP Images, p. 4; Mark J. Terrill/AP Images, p. 6; Patrick Semansky/AP Images, p. 7 (Jose Altuve); Red Line Editorial, pp. 7 (chart), 14; Gino Santa Maria/Shutterstock Images, p. 8; Kyodo/AP Images, p. 9; Keeton Gale/Shutterstock Images, pp. 10–11, 16; Luis Gutierrez/AP Images, pp. 12–13; Larry Goren/Four Seam Images/ AP Images, p. 15; Michael Wyke/AP Images, p. 17; Juan Carlos Hernandez/AP Images, p. 19; Erik Williams/Cal Sport Media/AP Images, pp. 20–21; travelview/Shutterstock Images, p. 21; Mike Flippo/Shutterstock Images, pp. 22, 25 (top); David J. Phillip/AP Images, p. 23; Charlie Riedel/AP Images, p. 24; KonstantinChristian/Shutterstock Images, pp. 25 (bottom), 30; Eric Christian Smith/AP Images, pp. 26–27.

ABOUT THE AUTHOR

Anthony K. Hewson is a freelance writer originally from San Diego, now living in the Bay Area with his wife and their two dogs.

DALLAS MAVERICKS

DEREK MOON

WWW.APEXEDITIONS.COM

Copyright © 2026 by Apex Editions, Mendota Heights, MN 55120. All rights reserved. No part of this book may be reproduced or utilized in any form or by any means without written permission from the publisher. No part of this book may be used or reproduced in any manner for the purpose of training artificial intelligence technologies or systems.

Apex is distributed by North Star Editions:
sales@northstareditions.com | 888-417-0195

Produced for Apex by Red Line Editorial.

Photographs ©: Marty Jean-Louis/Sipa USA/AP Images, cover, 1; Ron Jenkins/Getty Images Sport/Getty Images, 4–5, 42–43; LM Otero/AP Images, 6–7; Focus On Sport/Getty Images Sport/Getty Images, 8–9, 14–15, 19, 24–25; AP Images, 10–11; Eric Gay/AP Images, 12–13; Lisa Blumenfeld/Getty Images Sport/Getty Images, 16–17; Rick Stewart/Getty Images Sport/Getty Images, 20–21; Layne Murdoch/Getty Images Sport/Getty Images, 22–23; Tom Hauck/Allsport/Getty Images Sport/Getty Images, 26–27; Tony Gutierrez/AP Images, 29, 57; Brian Bahr/Getty Images Sport/Getty Images, 30–31; Tom DiPace/AP Images, 32–33, 58–59; Ronald Martinez/Getty Images Sport/Getty Images, 34–35; Matthew Stockman/Getty Images Sport/Getty Images, 36–37; Rob Carr/Getty Images Sport/Getty Images, 38–39; Christian Petersen/Getty Images Sport/Getty Images, 40–41; Justin Casterline/Getty Images Sport/Getty Images, 44–45; Tim Heitman/Getty Images Sport/Getty Images, 47, 48–49; Shutterstock Images, 50–51; Todd Kirkland/Getty Images Sport/Getty Images, 52–53; Richard Rodriguez/Getty Images Sport/Getty Images, 54–55

Library of Congress Control Number: 2025939632

ISBN
979-8-89250-899-5 (hardcover)
979-8-89250-930-5 (paperback)
979-8-89824-006-6 (ebook pdf)
979-8-89250-961-9 (hosted ebook)

Printed in the United States of America
Mankato, MN
012026

NOTE TO PARENTS AND EDUCATORS

Apex books are designed to build literacy skills in striving readers. Exciting, high-interest content attracts and holds readers' attention. The text is carefully leveled to allow students to achieve success quickly.